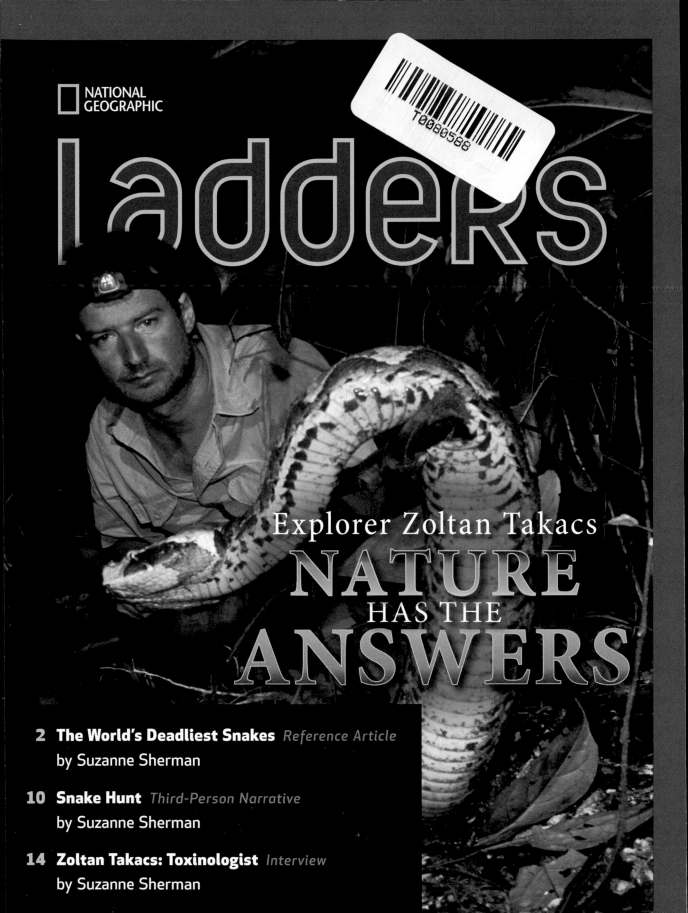

NATIONAL GEOGRAPHIC

ladders

Explorer Zoltan Takacs

NATURE HAS THE ANSWERS

GENRE Reference Article

Read to find out about some of the world's venomous snakes.

THE WORLD'S DEADLIEST SNAKES

by Suzanne Sherman

What animals are ferocious predators that can take down prey many times their size, without the help of arms or legs? Snakes! These scaled, streamlined reptiles swallow their meals whole. Depending on the species of snake, that meal could be a darting fish, a jumping frog, or even an antelope! How do they do it? Some species use strong muscles to surround and suffocate large prey to death. Others use a toxic mixture of chemicals called **venom.** One bite from a venomous snake can stop a large or fast-moving animal in its tracks.

Although most snakes avoid people, millions of people are bitten each year worldwide. Venomous species that cause the most snake bites and deaths easily make the list of "deadliest" snakes. Others deserve mention simply because of the amazing power of their venom!

Range and Habitat: African savanna

Venom Targets: Circulatory and nervous systems

Prey: Rodents

BLACK MAMBA

Dendroaspis polylepsis

The black mamba is actually grey or olive, with a light-colored belly. Only the inside of its mouth is ink black. The highly toxic and fast-acting venom of the black mamba enables it to prey on quick rodents. The venom also makes its bites among the most dangerous.

INLAND TAIPAN

Oxyuranus microlepidotus

Also called the "fierce snake," the inland taipan is a brown, medium to large snake with a dark, angular head. Although bites of people are unheard of, the inland taipan has the most toxic venom of any land snake. The venom from one snake bite has the capacity to kill 220,000 mice. Luckily, people rarely encounter this snake because of its remote habitat deep in central Australia.

Range and Habitat:
Central Australian plains

Venom Targets:
Nervous system, muscles, blood

Prey: Rodents

COMMON INDIAN KRAIT

Bungarus caeruleus

Some say the common Indian krait has dual personalities—shy during the day, active at night. This nocturnal hunter has a terrifying behavior of entering people's houses, burrowing under their blankets, and biting them while they are sleeping! Because the bite is painless, people may not realize they have been bitten. They may wake up paralyzed, or never wake up at all. This snake causes a large number of deaths in South Asia, where many people sleep on mats on the floor.

Range and Habitat:
Lowland Asia

Venom Target:
Nervous system

Prey: Snakes and sometimes other small animals

HOOK-NOSED SEA SNAKE

Enhydrina schistosa

The hook-nosed sea snake is one of the deadliest snakes that lives in water. The potent venom of the hook-nosed sea snake paralyzes its prey—here a pufferfish—before it can make an escape. This deadly snake is responsible for many fatal sea snake bites. It comes into contact with people fishing in its murky, shallow-water habitat.

Range and Habitat:
Indian and Pacific Ocean estuaries

Venom Targets:
Nervous system, muscles

Prey: Pufferfish and catfish

VENOMOUS, NOT POISONOUS

Venomous and *poisonous* are the same thing, right? Actually, they're not. Venomous animals inject harmful substances, or **toxins,** directly into their victims by biting or stinging them. Poisonous plants and animals, such as the poison dart frog, must be eaten or touched to inflict harm.

MAKING ANTIVENOM

In areas where good healthcare is available, snake bite victims can receive **antivenom.** Antivenom counteracts the effects of venom and can make the difference between life and death. Although antivenom has been developed for most species of snakes that cause medical problems, there are shortages worldwide.

‹ A man is paralyzed after being bitten by a cobra in rural Nepal. No antivenom is available there. Air must be hand-pumped into his lungs to keep him alive.

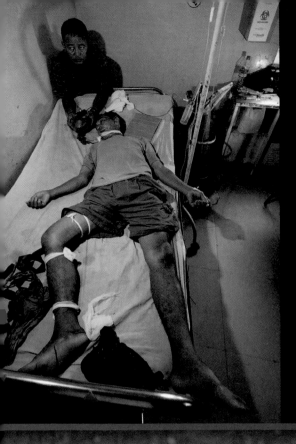

CARPET VIPER
Echis carinatus

Naming one snake as the "deadliest" is impossible because there are different ways to define "deadly." But certainly the carpet viper ranks high on the danger list. The carpet viper sometimes lies partially buried under the sand, awaiting its prey. This behavior makes the snake dangerously easy to step on, especially at night. Carpet vipers are responsible for more human deaths than any other snakes.

Range and Habitat:
Deserts of Middle East and central Asia

Venom Target:
Blood cells

Prey: Varied

TO MAKE ANTIVENOM:

1. A snake is "milked" of its venom. To milk a snake, the snake is given a vial to bite down on. Venom drips from its fangs and collects in the vial.

2. The venom is freeze-dried for storage and transport.

3. A small amount of venom is injected into a large animal, such as a horse.

4. The horse's body wages an immune response to the venom, producing substances in its blood that are extracted and used to make the antivenom.

Range and Habitat:
Asian forests and plains
Venom Target:
Nervous system
Prey: Mostly snakes

KING COBRA
Ophiophagus hannah

Spanning up to five and a half meters in length (almost 18 feet), the notorious king cobra is the longest venomous snake. It is also very dangerous, releasing enough venom in one bite to kill an elephant. When threatened, the king cobra flares its famous hood. King cobras live deep in forests away from humans.

TIGER RATTLESNAKE

Crotalus tigris

Rattlesnakes are venomous vipers found only in the Americas. Of all rattlesnakes, the tiger rattlesnake's venom is believed to be the most potent. Snake rattles are hard, empty segments made of the same material as our fingernails. When shaken, several of these segments knock against each other, making the rattle sound. The rattlesnake's message is clear: stay away!

Range and Habitat: Deserts and foothills of southwestern North America

Venom Target: Nervous system

Prey: Rodents and small reptiles

Range and Habitat: Mainly grasslands of Asia

Venom Targets: Nervous system, blood, and muscles

Prey: Rodents

RUSSELL'S VIPER

Daboia russelii

Each bite of the Russell's viper delivers a large amount of strong venom. Its namesake is Patrick Russell, a naturalist who first studied Indian snakes. Because this menacing viper eats rodents, it commonly lives near humans and in rice paddy fields. Along with kraits and cobras, the Russell's viper is a major cause of snake bite deaths in South Asia.

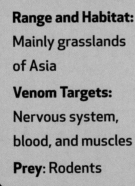

HOW FANGS WORK

Vipers have the longest fangs of any venomous snake. They can fold away when not in use.

venom duct

nostril

Venom is produced and stored in two venom glands inside the cheeks. When the snake bites, muscles around the glands compress and venom is squeezed through the venom ducts into the fangs.

venom canal

Venom moves through the venom canals to the fangs. Cobra and viper fangs are grooved or hollow, allowing venom to flow all the way to the tips and be injected deep into their prey, like a doctor's needle.

tongue

The jaws of snakes are not fused together, so they can expand their mouths enough to swallow food bigger than their own heads.

A tube called the glottis allows snakes to breathe even when they have large prey in their mouths.

Check In What advantages do venomous snakes have over other species of snakes?

GENRE Third-Person Narrative

Read to find out why Zoltan Takacs chases down deadly snakes.

Snake Hunt

by Suzanne Sherman

ZOLTAN TAKACS is a National Geographic Explorer, herpetologist, and toxinologist. That means he is a scientist working to understand the **venoms** of animals, especially snakes. Born in Hungary, Zoltan's adventurous spirit and passion for snakes has taken him to remote locations in 138 different countries. His daring expeditions and exciting research have been featured in several magazines and TV programs.

With his face whipped by wind and his hand steadying the outboard motor of a small boat, Zoltan Takacs gazes out over an endless series of waves. He is in the South Pacific Ocean, scanning the waters for dangerous sea snakes. His goal is not to avoid the snakes, but to catch them. Zoltan journeys to the far corners of Earth in search of venomous snakes. He goes scuba diving in shark-infested waters, trekking through rain forests, and camping in deserts. His mission: to collect venom samples from as many species as possible to bring back to his lab, where they may be used to make new life-saving medicines.

Zoltan combines his expertise with local people's knowledge to find the snakes. He knows that, like all reptiles, sea snakes need to breathe air. Because sea snakes are prevalent in this area, he expects that one will eventually come to the surface to breathe.

With thick protective gloves already pulled over his hands, Zoltan is ready to make a move. Suddenly, he sees a faint line weaving in and out of view, just beneath the water's surface. It's a snake! Zoltan leaps into the water. Within seconds, Zoltan deftly grabs a snake and lifts it out of the water with one hand. Soon, he pulls up two more snakes with his other hand! Ever so cautiously, he swims the snakes back to his boat and puts them in a bag.

ack ashore, Zoltan removes a boldly black-and-white striped snake from the bag. It is a yellow-lipped sea krait, a snake that lives in the ocean but lays its eggs on land.

The yellow-lipped sea krait possesses one of the most toxic venoms known. Zoltan knows this species rarely bites, but he is extremely careful nonetheless as he handles this highly venomous animal. Zoltan is acutely aware of the danger in his work. Three of his friends have died from snake bites.

Snakes are even more perilous to Zoltan than to most people, because he is allergic to their venom and the life-saving **antivenom.** However, through hard work that he loves to do, he has gained 30 years of experience in venomous snake handling.

Zoltan carefully reaches toward the sea krait with a stick, quickly pinning the snake to the ground, just behind its head. Then he securely grasps the back of the snake's head with his own hand. His fingers are safely shielded yet only millimeters away from the snake's deadly fangs.

Zoltan often travels by himself. He carries only a backpack with camping gear, a camera, and sample-collecting kit.

Wearing thick gloves, Zoltan reaches for a venomous sea snake.

Zoltan carefully holds the head of the sea krait as he obtains a blood sample.

Before he can release the snake, he must obtain a sample in the form of tissue, such as a venom gland or blood. Tissue contains the **DNA,** or the body's chemical instructions, for making **toxins.** Toxins are harmful substances found in the snake's venom. Surprisingly, toxins can also lead to new medicines. There are already about a dozen kinds of medicine based on toxins from animal venoms. These drugs are used to treat a variety of conditions, from high blood pressure and heart attacks to diabetes and pain. With more than 100,000 venomous species out there, Zoltan believes many more new medicines are possible.

To get a blood sample, Zoltan turns the snake upside down and locates its beating heart. There, he inserts a small needle and draws a couple of drops of blood. Then he releases the snake back into the ocean with no lasting damage.

Zoltan gathers his gear and continues on his expedition, excited about his collection. He can't wait to get back to his lab to analyze the sample. The toxins he collected today may save lives tomorrow.

Check In Why does Zoltan collect the blood samples of venomous snakes?

GENRE Interview   **Read to find out** about the work of a toxin scientist.

Zoltan Takac

TOXINOLOGIST

by Suzanne Sherman

If you didn't think a scientist could **engineer new molecules** on some days and fly airplanes and **dive for lethal snakes** on other days, then you have never met **Zoltan Takacs.**

As a boy in Hungary, Zoltan Takacs embarked on wild adventures with his friends, chasing snakes, and sometimes even bringing them home into his bedroom. Now as an adult, he has made snakes a central part of his career. Zoltan followed his passion and became a scientist, explorer, and world expert in snake **venom.**

After Zoltan returns from his expeditions, he brings blood samples from the snakes back to his research lab where he tries to uncover their secrets. In his lab, he uses the latest technology to analyze the venom's harmful substances, called **toxins.** He wants to know what potential they may hold for making new medicines. To Zoltan, analyzing venom is like opening a present, because he never knows what he will find "inside."

Each species' venom is a concoction of toxins that act on, or target, different vital parts of the body. Some toxins target nerve cells, others target muscle cells, and still others disrupt blood flow. Because toxins selectively affect their targets, medicine made from the toxins might not cause many unwanted side effects.

To learn more about this exciting work, read an interview with Zoltan himself, starting on the next page.

Zoltan inspects a viper at the home of his host in Panama.

A heart attack patient's artery is clogged. Blood can't flow through it.

Identifying and Describing the Problem

National Geographic: What inspired you to study snake venom?

Zoltan Takacs: I'm fascinated with nature. I love beauty and the unknown, and with snakes, you find both. Since kindergarten, I have been catching and keeping reptiles. Searching for them and finding them was exciting. Discovering how they feed, lay eggs, and hibernate was absolutely amazing. In high school,

I caught my first viper. A few months later, I had to save my friend's life with **antivenom** after a snake bite that happened while we were alone in the mountains catching snakes. The next year, I had my own first snake bite, and had to save my own life.

What could have been more interesting to a kid than exploring mysteries in far away places? I got a great education,

Normal blood thickens after 20 minutes (left). Blood drawn from a viper-bitten patient loses its ability to thicken (right). This effect is harmful to snake bite victims but useful in medicine.

A drug based on viper venom allows blood to flow through the artery again. The patient's life is saved.

and I learned to scuba dive and fly airplanes to support my quests.

Today, the overall goal is to develop new drugs from venoms. Toxins are excellent templates to make drugs because nature has been perfecting them for millions of years. They are highly specific—they target only one or very few critical parts of the body. And they are very potent—you need a very small amount to have a biological effect.

NG: Why do you collect samples from many different species?

Zoltan Takacs: Venoms have been perfected over millions of years, in over a hundred thousand different animals, in different ecosystems: in the rain forests, in the deserts, deep in the seas. So that diversity produced a great variety of toxins, each with unique properties. One species has a totally different set of toxins than another one. Different toxins mean more medical potential.

Engineering Solutions

National Geographic: Why do you collect blood samples rather than venom samples?

Zoltan Takacs: I collect venom, but I collect venom from snake tissues. The tissue can be a venom gland or blood, or even a piece of skin shed by a snake. All these tissues contain **DNA.** DNA is the complete blueprint for making the toxin. Unlike "milked venom," DNA withstands travel in tropical heat.

Once DNA is sequenced, the information can be stored on a hard drive. Then you can use bacteria to make unlimited amounts of the original toxin.

NG: How do you analyze the samples?

Zoltan Takacs: We sequence the DNA. When we do this, we reveal the secrets locked into the toxins. It's a very cool privilege to see that firsthand. Then we analyze what toxins do to their target.

Zoltan looks to nature for solutions.
He studies the DNA of venomous
animals including scorpions and snakes.

NG: In what ways do you use engineering and math skills in your research?

Zoltan Takacs: We use a wide range of sciences and technology. We need to rebuild nature's toxins in the lab. We must alter them as we wish. We must command bacteria and viruses to make the toxins for us, so we can experiment with them. We need to detect and measure what they do and how well they do it.

All this requires knowledge of science and engineering skills. When you design an airplane, you have to know what keeps it in the air. We do similar things at a level that is so small it is invisible to the eye, but doable for scientists.

Math is everywhere. We measure, calculate, convert, and predict things all the time. We're working with numbers from the *nano*, or very small numbers, all the way up to the *yotta*, which are very large numbers.

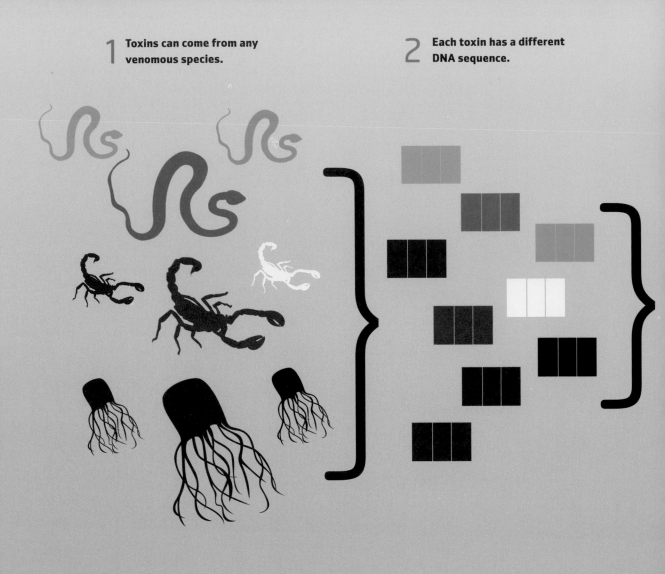

1 Toxins can come from any venomous species.

2 Each toxin has a different DNA sequence.

Designing and Improving Solutions

National Geographic: Tell me about a new technology that you are developing.

Zoltan Takacs: We have 20 million toxins in nature. To screen, or test, all those toxins by traditional methods would take forever. My colleagues and I invented "designer toxins." This technology allows thousands to millions of toxins to be screened at once to see which one has a desirable effect for medicine.

Not only can we screen nature's original toxins, but we can engineer and screen variations of the toxins. For example, we can fuse three snake toxins to make a new artificial toxin. Or, we can combine a scorpion, snake, and snail toxin into one new toxin. Using the designer toxin

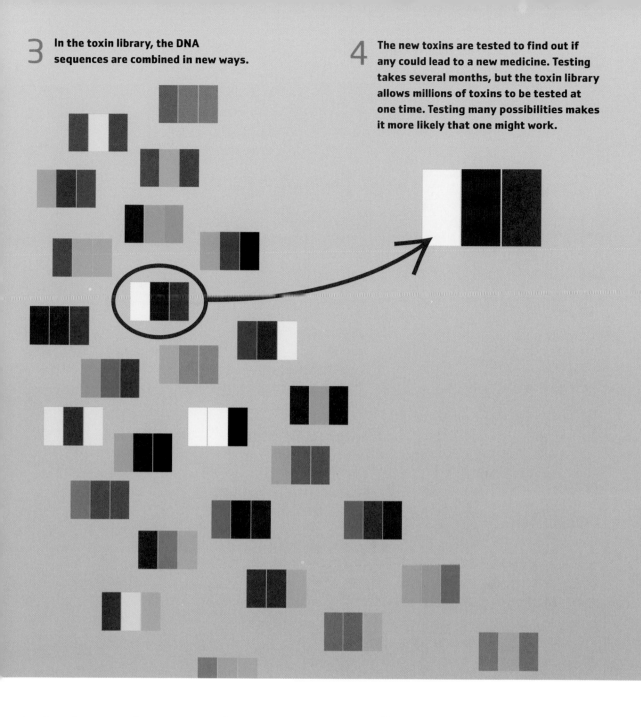

3 In the toxin library, the DNA sequences are combined in new ways.

4 The new toxins are tested to find out if any could lead to a new medicine. Testing takes several months, but the toxin library allows millions of toxins to be tested at one time. Testing many possibilities makes it more likely that one might work.

technology, we have created a vast library of toxins. With so many toxins to screen, the chance of finding the one with medical value goes very high.

NG: How have your ideas changed and improved?

Zoltan Takacs: In science, as we learn new information, our ideas, goals, and methods constantly evolve. But the overall aim stays the same. We want to understand and appreciate nature. We identify problems, raise new questions, and use new tools.

We also have failures. Failure is perfectly normal. It can actually help you, because by understanding the cause of the failure and how it affected your work, you can perfect whatever you are working on.

Zoltan looks at a computer model of a new toxin made from combining three scorpion toxins. The toxin may lead to a new medicine.

Results

National Geographic: What results have come from your work so far?

Zoltan Takacs: As a result of our new designer toxin technology, we can create and screen thousands or millions of new toxin variations for medical application. We have produced new toxins that look very promising at this stage. They may have the potential to treat immune system disorders, such as multiple sclerosis, arthritis, or diabetes.

NG: What are your future plans in venom research?

Zoltan Takacs: We are expanding and perfecting our technology to harness toxins aimed at different diseases. There are so many toxins out there, it is like exploring a gold mine. In some way, we are racing against the loss of **biodiversity.** Once species are lost, we may lose millions of years of natural "wisdom" locked into their toxins. That is, we may lose a cure or treatment for a disease.

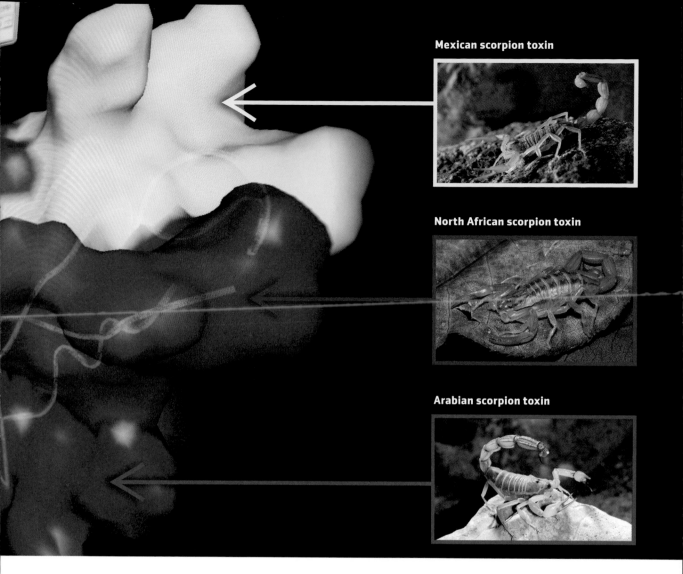

Mexican scorpion toxin

North African scorpion toxin

Arabian scorpion toxin

NG: What would you suggest to students who are interested in biology?

Zoltan Takacs: Follow your dreams and passion. You must love what you are doing. Get a strong education in biology and all other fields of science. Don't shy away from questions and problems. Addressing them will make you smarter and more prepared. Get out and travel. Observe and understand how nature works. Listen to smart people's advice, even if you don't always follow the advice.

Be open. Explore new things. When I was in high school, at age 14, my friends and I went to Bulgaria to look for snakes by ourselves. Bulgaria is two countries away from my native Hungary. We collected many snakes. I still have toxin samples from that trip.

Make full use of the learning tools you have. Use technology to retrieve images from deep in Africa, or stay in touch with conservation biologists in India. Instead of watching TV, go out and shoot your own movie of a frog or snake.

Check In What do you think Zoltan meant by, "We are racing against a loss of biodiversity?"

Read to find out how toxins from diverse creatures are leading to new medicines.

The World's

The next treatment for your aches and pains may be lurking in the ocean, hiding in the desert, or hopping in the rain forest. In **biodiversity**, nature may hold the keys to solving many medical problems. A great variety of living things around the planet produce **toxins** to help them survive in

Answers for Pain

Cone Snail

Venom from the cone snail contains about 100 different toxins. One toxin that acts on nerve cells is leading to a new pain medicine that is a thousand times stronger than existing pain medicines and is not addictive.

MORE ABOUT THE ANIMAL

- Cone snails dwell in tropical ocean habitats worldwide.

- The sting of a cone snail can be deadly, even to humans.

- Cone snails paralyze their prey by striking them with a venom-loaded tooth. The tooth is shot out of a long tube.

- Wild populations of cone snails are under threat from habitat destruction and collectors after their patterned shells.

Laboratory

by Suzanne Sherman

their environments. These toxins and other substances are leading to exciting new directions in medicine. Prepare to be "stunned" as you read about these amazing creatures and the potential uses of their toxins.

Poison Dart Frog

A toxin from the skin of the brightly colored poison dart frog may lead to a potent new pain medicine. A human-made version of the toxin has promise in treating pain without the unwanted side effects of other pain medicines.

MORE ABOUT THE ANIMAL

- Poison dart frogs live in the tropical rain forests of Central and South America.

- More than 100 species of poison dart frogs display a range of colors including bright red, brilliant gold, and deep blue. The vibrant colors serve as a warning to predators of their high toxicity.

- Male poison dart frogs are devoted dads; they carry eggs and tadpoles on their backs.

- Several species are endangered because of rain forest destruction.

Sea Anemone

A sea anemone toxin may be the key to treating multiple sclerosis (MS). People with multiple sclerosis slowly lose feeling in limbs, and function of their bodies. A new medicine based on the sea anemone toxin may be able to stop, and actually reverse, the paralysis.

MORE ABOUT THE ANIMAL

• Sea anemones live at the bottom of the world's oceans, securely attached to rocks with one sticky foot.

• When prey passes by, anemones sting them with their array of venom-filled tentacles.

• The smallest species of sea anemone measures only a little over a centimeter (about a half inch). The largest spans nearly two meters (six feet).

Common Vampire Bat

A toxin from the vampire bat could give stroke patients more time to get life-saving treatment. The toxin, found in the bat's saliva, causes blood to flow more easily into the bat's mouth from its prey. Researchers discovered that a human-made version of the toxin dissolves blood clots in people. Blood clots can cause brain damage or death when they clog blood flow in the brain.

MORE ABOUT THE ANIMAL

- The common vampire bat lives in the tropics of North, Central, and South America. It feeds at night, mainly on cattle and horse blood.

- The teeth of the vampire bat are so sharp that its sleeping victim is rarely awakened by the bite.

Answers for the Heart

Chilean Rose Tarantula

A toxin from the Chilean rose tarantula may stop people from dying of heart attacks. During a heart attack, the heart can fibrillate, or beat wildly. This fibrillation can cause people to die because blood is not delivered to the body. Researchers found that a tarantula toxin can actually keep heart cells from fibrillating.

MORE ABOUT THE ANIMAL

- Wild Chilean rose tarantulas live in the deserts of South America where they feed on insects.

- Tarantulas rarely bite people. When they do, the bite symptoms are typically no worse than a bee sting.

Box Jellyfish

A box jellyfish toxin might make risky heart transplant operations safer. Researchers discovered that the jellyfish toxin temporarily stops the heart from beating. Once the toxin wears off, the heart comes back to life with no damage. The toxin could be applied to help replaced hearts recover fully.

MORE ABOUT THE ANIMAL

- Box jellyfish mainly live in the coastal waters of northern Australia.

- Box jellyfish have 24 eyes and no central brain. Yet they are skillful hunters.

- The jellyfish's highly toxic venom is delivered using tiny stinging cells on their tentacles. The tentacles dangle up to three meters in length (about 10 feet).

Pitcher Plant

A toxin from a tropical pitcher plant may lead to a better antifungal medicine. The medicine could treat athlete's foot. It could also help prevent infections that spread through hospitals and kill thousands each year.

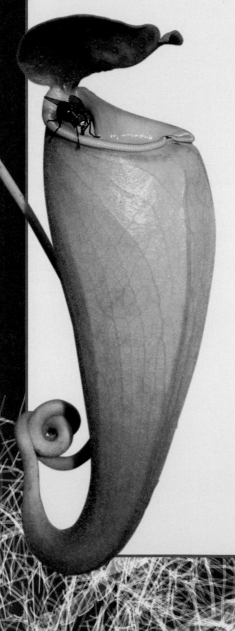

MORE ABOUT THE PLANT

- The tropical pitcher plant lives in tropical island habitats between Asia and Australia.

- The tropical pitcher plant is a carnivorous plant that feeds on unsuspecting animals! It traps its prey in a leaf filled with toxic liquids.

- Animals are drawn to the liquid's odor. They fall into the cup and can't get out. They are eventually digested by the plant's liquids.

- Many species of pitcher plants are in danger because of habitat destruction and collecting.

Spiny Starfish

A substance in the spiny starfish's slimy coating could fight conditions such as asthma. "Starfish," or sea stars, are not actually fish; they are related to sea urchins and sand dollars.

MORE ABOUT THE ANIMAL

- Spiny starfish live in coastal habitats. These habitats range from exposed rocks to mud.

- Spiny starfish can be blue, green, or purple. They are named for the thick spines that cover them.

- Like most sea stars, spiny starfish can grow back limbs that have been bitten off by a predator.

Check In Describe three medical problems that nature can help solve.

Discuss

1. Why do you think this book was titled *Nature Has the Answers*?

2. How do the structures of a viper's fangs help the viper survive?

3. Describe some way toxins hurt people and some ways they help people.

4. How might Zoltan's work lead to more discoveries like the ones described in "The World's Laboratory"?

5. What questions do you still have about using toxins to make medicine? What would be a good way to find out more information?